William Bligh
a stormy story of tempestuous times

Written by Michael Sedunary

Artwork by Bern Emmerichs

!

BERBAY
PUBLISHING

www.berbaybooks.com

For Jake, Oscar, Zac, Zoe, Mia,
Ollie and Lexi…all such grand kids!
MS

In memory of Chocolate and Charlie,
(horse and hound) our two hairy soulful
sons and brothers. For all the joy, love
and warmth you brought into our lives,
may you R.I.P. at Bergamo.
BE

First published by Berbay Publishing Pty Ltd, 2016
This edition published by Berbay Publishing Pty Ltd, 2016

Berbay Publishing Pty Ltd
PO Box 133 Kew East
Victoria 3102 Australia

1 3 5 7 9 10 8 6 4

Text © Michael Sedunary
Illustrations © Bern Emmerichs

Edited by Catherine McCredie
Designed by John Canty
Printed and bound in China
by Everbest Printing

Cataloguing-in publication data
available from the
National Library of Australia

ISBN 978-0-9942895-6-8

Visit our website www.berbaybooks.com

www.cleverkids.net.au

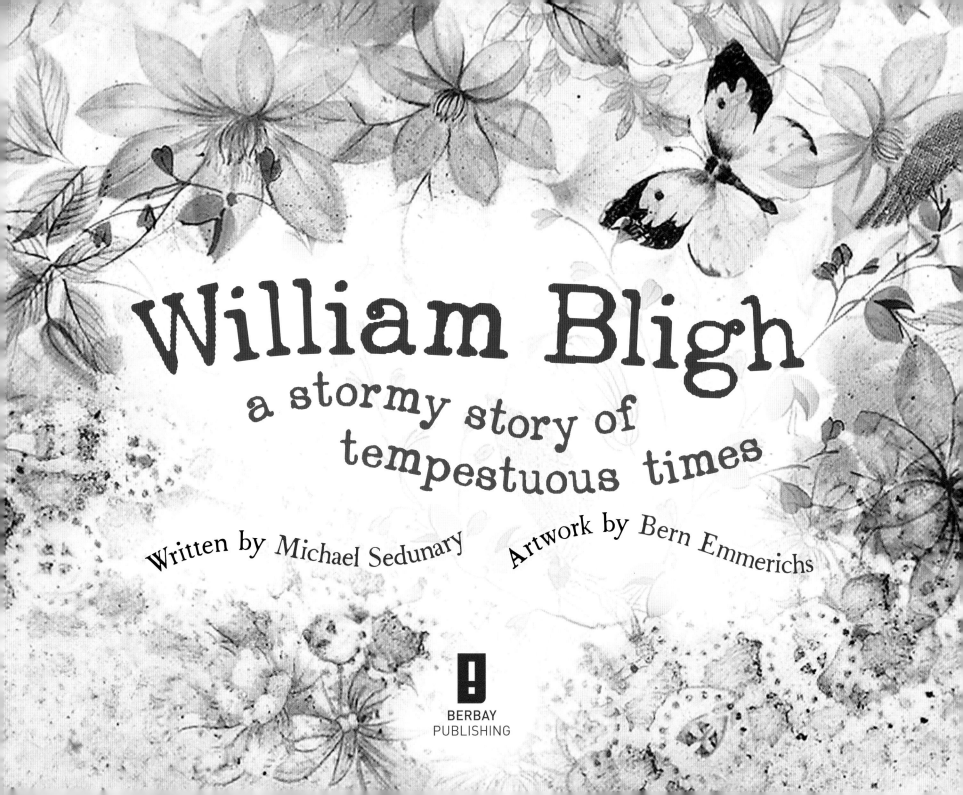

William Bligh

a stormy story of tempestuous times

Written by Michael Sedunary   Artwork by Bern Emmerichs

BERBAY
PUBLISHING

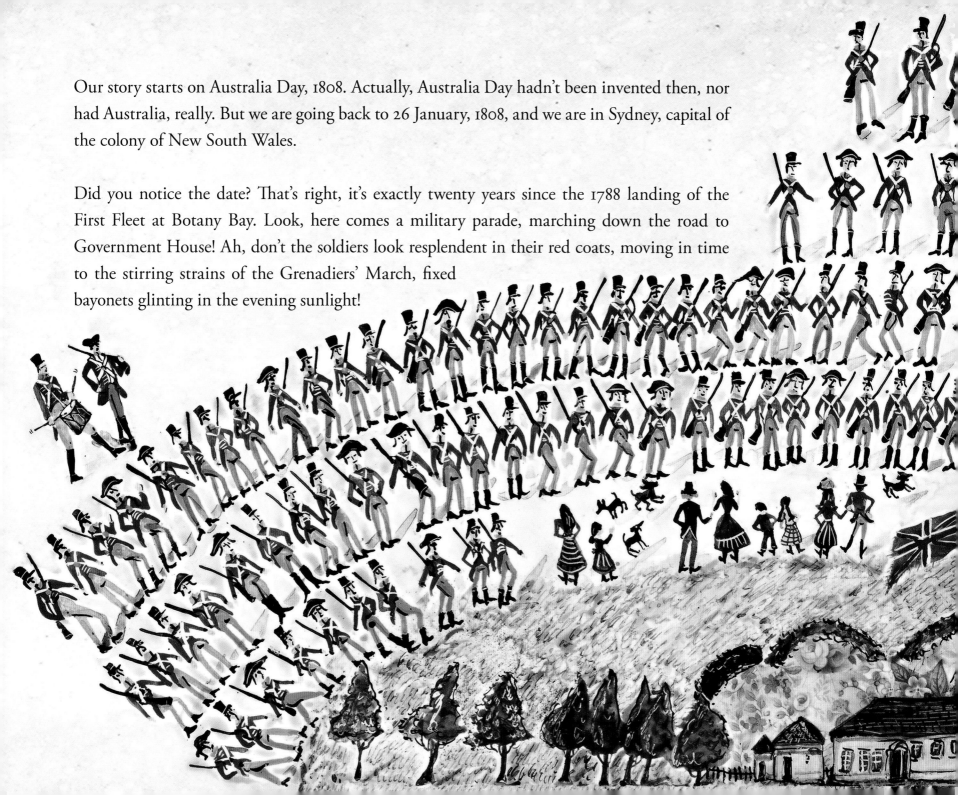

Our story starts on Australia Day, 1808. Actually, Australia Day hadn't been invented then, nor had Australia, really. But we are going back to 26 January, 1808, and we are in Sydney, capital of the colony of New South Wales.

Did you notice the date? That's right, it's exactly twenty years since the 1788 landing of the First Fleet at Botany Bay. Look, here comes a military parade, marching down the road to Government House! Ah, don't the soldiers look resplendent in their red coats, moving in time to the stirring strains of the Grenadiers' March, fixed bayonets glinting in the evening sunlight!

People have gathered to see what is going on. We can see a few children marching alongside the soldiers and a couple of dogs wheeling around in excited circles. But wait, who is that Aboriginal man leaning against a tree, observing these events? Could it be Bennelong, once a friend of the first governor, Arthur Phillip and ambassador for his people? He's no longer welcome at Government House, but he still comes into town every so often. What is he thinking?

The soldiers march on and sweep through the front gates of Government House.

But what's this? There's a young woman confronting the soldiers, trying to block their progress. She screams at them, 'You traitors, you rebels! You come to murder my father!'

This must be Mary, Governor Bligh's daughter. She came from England to look after him, and everyone knows she is very protective of her father. And look, now she is trying to fight them off with her parasol! That's feisty!

The soldiers look embarrassed and are not sure what to do until a couple of them are ordered to drag her aside. A few others rush into the house, with orders to arrest the governor. Bligh hears their footsteps and realises they are coming for him. He retreats to an upstairs bedroom and thinks, Do I stand on my dignity and confront them? Do I try to escape, to give myself a chance of winning back my authority?

Bligh hears the soldiers cursing as room after room turns out to be empty. His refuge is a bedroom where secret papers are stored and he is busily destroying the documents when two soldiers burst through the door and arrest him at bayonet point. As they march him downstairs, threatening him with death should he show any resistance, Bligh thinks to himself, No, not again. I don't believe it!

What was the earlier incident in Governor Bligh's mind? Let's go back to the dining room of his London house in 1787, when he was a 33-year-old lieutenant in the British Navy.

A group of men, who will soon be sailing under Bligh's command on HMS (His Majesty's Ship) *Bounty*, are dining with him. Their voyage will take them to the Pacific island of Tahiti where they will pick up hundreds of breadfruit plants to transport to British colonies in the West Indies. There the plants will be grown to provide cheap food for the slaves working on the sugar plantations.

More about that later, for the dining room door has opened and Bligh's wife, Elizabeth, has ushered in their three daughters to say goodnight to the guests. The eldest, Mary – she looks about five years old – gives a goodnight kiss to Fletcher Christian, a family friend. Christian will be the Master on the *Bounty*, which means he will be Bligh's second-in-command.

With Mary and her sisters tucked away in bed, the men go back to discussing their mission. As he listens, Bligh feels some satisfaction at being given this new command. With an impressive fighting record in naval battles against the French and experience as Captain Cook's Master on HMS *Resolution*, he feels he deserves it. Cook praised Bligh for his skills at drawing maps and charts, an important task in the days of world exploration.

There is one thing that irks him: why is he still just a lieutenant? Why has the Admiralty not promoted him to the rank of captain? His record speaks for itself! The *Bounty* voyage to Tahiti and beyond is extremely important and will require exceptional seamanship and diplomacy. He should be Captain Bligh!

A few months later at Portsmouth, about 100 kilometres from London, on the south coast of England, Lieutenant Bligh is standing on a dock in the harbour, looking at his new ship, the *Bounty*. It's not a large man-of-war, like the naval vessels he's used to sailing. It's a small ship really, with guns moved out to make room for the breadfruit plants it will be carrying. Things will be pretty cramped for the forty-six crew on board, but they will make the best of it.

Bligh is generally happy with his recruits, although he is concerned about Thomas Huggan, the ship's doctor, who has a reputation for drunkenness and sleeping on the job. And he will have to keep an eye on young Heywood, who, at fourteen, is two years younger than Bligh was when he joined the navy. And there is the fiddler, Michael Byrne, who is almost blind. He will have an important job once they get under way.

It is frustrating sitting in Portsmouth, waiting for fair winds to blow up and carry them out of the harbour to the South Seas. Most of the crew are already living on the ship, while Bligh spends time in town with his 'poor little family', as he calls them, who have come down from London to see him off.

HMS *Bounty* sets sail on 28 November 1787. As the green fields of Hampshire fade into the background, does Bligh order Michael Byrne to stand on deck and play 'Rule Britannia'?

dance dance

BOUNTY

Fair sailing winds do not last forever and soon the *Bounty* runs into fierce storms. The able seamen on board are battered by winds and swamped by waves as they fight to keep the ship on course. A couple report to the doctor with serious rib and shoulder injuries but he is not competent, or sober, enough to help them. Crew morale dives when barrels containing their beer supply are washed overboard.

Much of the sailors' food, salted and pickled, is kept in barrels too. The job of rationing the food to make it last the whole voyage falls to the ship's purser, and in the case of the *Bounty* this is the captain, William Bligh.

Bligh is very disciplined and it is not long before hungry men, glaring at the small helpings on their plates, are cursing him under their breath. Rumours circulate about lavish feasts in the captain's cabin.

Conditions are cramped. Thirty of the forty-six men sleep in a space measuring about 10 by 6 metres, with headroom of only 170 centimetres. At 176 centimetres in height, Fletcher Christian has to stoop whenever he enters this stuffy and smelly area.

Bligh recognises the stresses of shipboard life, the dangers of living for months in such confined conditions and the need for regular exercise. He has a plan, as he writes in his captain's log: 'Some time for relaxation and mirth is absolutely necessary, and I have considered it so much so, that after four o'clock, the evening is laid aside for their amusement and dancing.'

That's right, dancing! Late each afternoon Michael Byrne takes out his fiddle and plays reels and hornpipes while the sailors dance – whether they feel like it or not. Bligh does not take kindly to his orders being disobeyed, so when John Mills and William Brown refuse to dance he stops their allowance of rum.

"All this morning has been spent drying wet clothes and airing and cleaning below... It is all I can do to keep the people's accommodation clean and

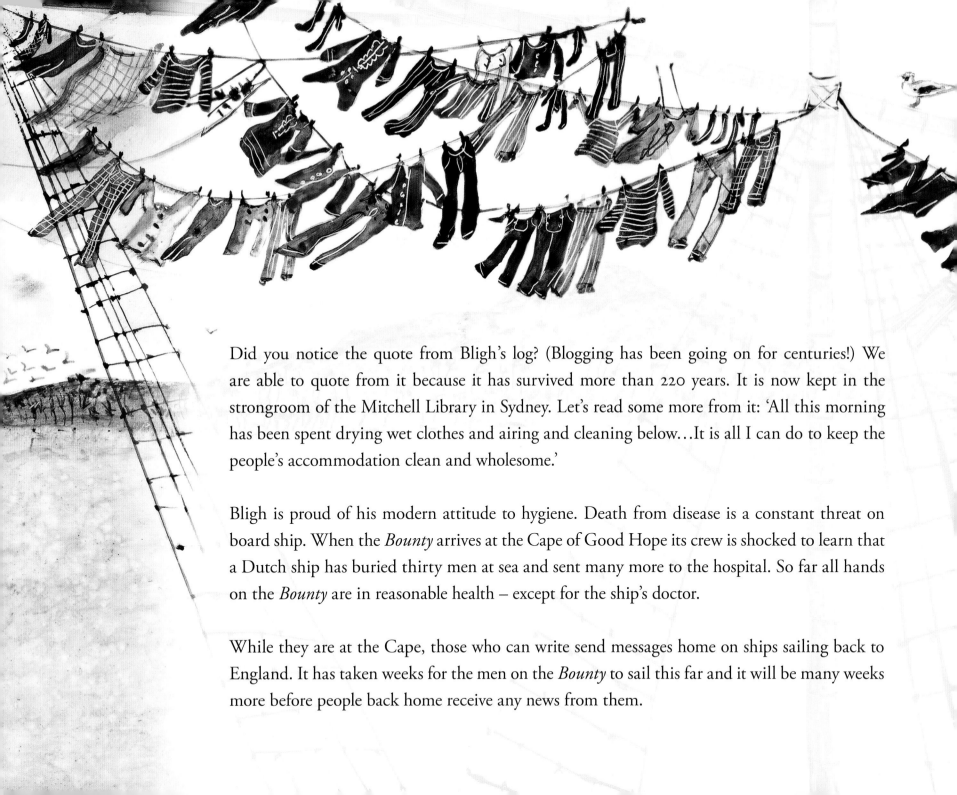

Did you notice the quote from Bligh's log? (Blogging has been going on for centuries!) We are able to quote from it because it has survived more than 220 years. It is now kept in the strongroom of the Mitchell Library in Sydney. Let's read some more from it: 'All this morning has been spent drying wet clothes and airing and cleaning below…It is all I can do to keep the people's accommodation clean and wholesome.'

Bligh is proud of his modern attitude to hygiene. Death from disease is a constant threat on board ship. When the *Bounty* arrives at the Cape of Good Hope its crew is shocked to learn that a Dutch ship has buried thirty men at sea and sent many more to the hospital. So far all hands on the *Bounty* are in reasonable health – except for the ship's doctor.

While they are at the Cape, those who can write send messages home on ships sailing back to England. It has taken weeks for the men on the *Bounty* to sail this far and it will be many weeks more before people back home receive any news from them.

Before we land the *Bounty* at Tahiti, let's consider a challenging aspect of shipboard life, namely that of discipline and punishment.

Bligh writes in his log: 'I had hopes I could have performed the voyage without punishment to anyone, but I found it necessary to punish Matthew Quintal with two dozen lashes for insolence and contempt.' Now, twenty-four lashes with the cat-o'-nine-tails is harsh punishment and we understand why a captain who cares about his men's welfare would be reluctant to use it. It would not happen today. But attitudes change over time and this was standard naval discipline in the eighteenth and nineteenth centuries. For that matter, it was not too many years ago that the cane and the strap were commonly used in our schools. Ask a grandparent!

Today, Bligh is often thought of as a brutal tyrant who enjoyed making his men suffer. Much of this is due to Hollywood versions of the *Bounty* story. If you look at some of the DVD covers of the 1935 movie *Mutiny on the Bounty*, you will see a leering, sneering, sinister movie villain. A 1962 remake of the movie reaffirmed the myth.

However, there is no evidence that Bligh used excessive flogging for his time, or that he ordered anyone to be keelhauled (dragged under water from one end of the ship to the other) or 'masted' (forced to climb ropes to the top of the mast and stay there for an extended period). In fact, Captain Cook ordered far more floggings than Bligh ever did. Yet to many, one is a hero, the other a villain.

MATTHEW QUINTAL "insolence and contempt"

Fast forward to HMS *Bounty* anchoring off the coast of the island of Tahiti. It has been an exhausting voyage of eleven months, so all on board are filled with relief and optimism as they watch the Tahitian natives paddling their canoes out towards their ship.

Bligh and his crew have heard accounts from other mariners such as Captain Cook of the warm welcome given to those who drop anchor at Tahiti, and they are not disappointed. Celebration is in the air as the locals board the *Bounty* and exchange presents. The sailors' eyes are caught by the beauty of Tahitian women, who are not hampered by excessive clothing, like the women in cold, grey London were.

Now begins the most delicate part of Bligh's mission: to convince Tinah, the local chief, to give him and his men dozens of breadfruit plants. This will require diplomacy and tact, and not a little cultural sensitivity.

Bligh showers the chief with presents: tools such as hatchets and saws, and trinkets such as mirrors and red feathers. For Tinah's wife there are earrings, necklaces and beads. He insists that all these gifts come from the great English king, George III, and that His Majesty would very much appreciate the breadfruit plants in return.

Tinah agrees to this exchange, but tells Bligh something that none of the botanists back home knew: this is not the season to transplant the breadfruit. He will have to wait until the plants have finished fruiting, in five months' time!

24 Dec 1788 ← 1787

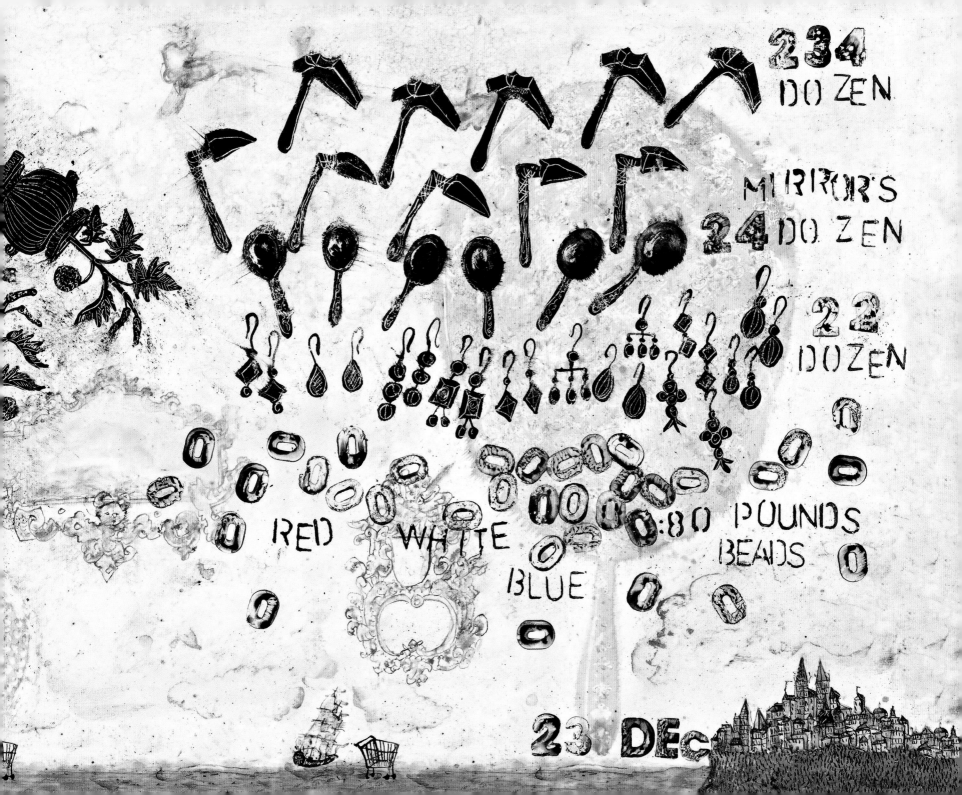

234
DO ZEN

MIRROR'S
24 DO ZEN

22
DOZEN

RED   WHITE   :80 POUNDS

BLUE   BEADS

23 DEC

So here they all are, 'trapped' in a tropical island paradise for five months. The appeal of Tahiti is irresistible: the brilliant sunlight, the energising warmth, the deep clear water of the lagoons, the luscious fruit hanging from the trees. What a contrast to the dull, damp climate they came from and the spartan conditions on the *Bounty*.

In his log, Bligh writes of 'the friendly and endearing behaviour of these people'. How pleasing are the attentions of these charming women and welcoming men after the drudgery and discipline of shipboard life! How sinuous and sensuous are their dances compared with the sailors' own clumsy clumping on deck!

Bligh is having trouble enforcing discipline in this balmy environment. His officers are distracted from their duties and neglecting even basic tasks. Bligh is shocked to discover that his orders to air and dry the *Bounty*'s sails have been ignored. Rotting sails could put their whole onward voyage at risk.

In his log, Bligh reflects on the disobedience of his men: 'Their conduct in general is so bad… they have driven me to everything but corporal punishment [flogging], and that must follow if they do not improve.'

When three of his men steal one of the *Bounty*'s small boats, load it up with arms and ammunition, and row it away, Bligh responds quickly. With the help of some natives, he recaptures the deserters – for that is what they are – and sentences them to twelve or twenty-four lashes. Bligh also punishes the officer who was asleep on his watch when the boat was stolen.

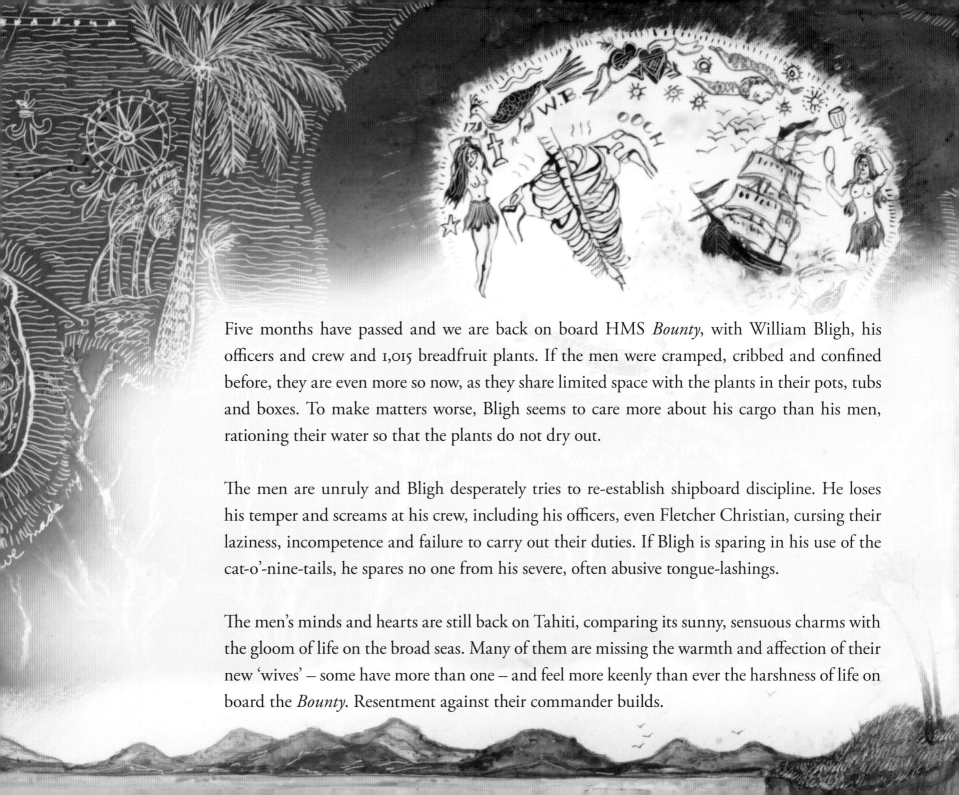

Five months have passed and we are back on board HMS *Bounty*, with William Bligh, his officers and crew and 1,015 breadfruit plants. If the men were cramped, cribbed and confined before, they are even more so now, as they share limited space with the plants in their pots, tubs and boxes. To make matters worse, Bligh seems to care more about his cargo than his men, rationing their water so that the plants do not dry out.

The men are unruly and Bligh desperately tries to re-establish shipboard discipline. He loses his temper and screams at his crew, including his officers, even Fletcher Christian, cursing their laziness, incompetence and failure to carry out their duties. If Bligh is sparing in his use of the cat-o'-nine-tails, he spares no one from his severe, often abusive tongue-lashings.

The men's minds and hearts are still back on Tahiti, comparing its sunny, sensuous charms with the gloom of life on the broad seas. Many of them are missing the warmth and affection of their new 'wives' – some have more than one – and feel more keenly than ever the harshness of life on board the *Bounty*. Resentment against their commander builds.

It is 28 April 1789, twenty-four days since the *Bounty* sailed from Tahiti. Just before sunrise, Fletcher Christian and a small band of others burst into Bligh's cabin while he is fast asleep and, holding naked bayonets to his heart, threaten him with death if he makes a noise. They haul their commander out of bed and force him on deck, hands tied painfully behind his back.

Ignoring the threats, Bligh cries out for assistance from his officers. But this mutiny is well organised: those not taking part in the conspiracy have armed guards at their cabin doors. As he stands on deck, Bligh again tries to rally support but he is greeted with shouts of, 'Damn his eyes, blow his brains out!'

When they are not threatening their captain, the mutineers are cheering, 'Huzzah for Tahiti!'

The mutineers lower the *Bounty*'s launch to the water and order those they consider loyal to Bligh into it. The captain tries to reason with the mutineers, but Christian shouts over him, 'Not a word, Sir, or you are dead this instant!'

As the men force Bligh onto the launch he reminds Christian of his many acts of kindness, including a promise to see Christian promoted once they return to England. Christian looks disturbed and says, 'That, Captain Bligh, that is the thing; I am in Hell – I am in Hell!' Any more words from Christian are drowned out by the cheering of the others, 'Huzzah for Tahiti!'

Hell for Christian, high water for Bligh, as he is cast adrift in a small boat with eighteen others. And now begins one of the most remarkable sea voyages ever undertaken, worthy of a separate book of its own.

The *Bounty*'s launch is only seven metres long, two metres wide and less than a metre deep. With nineteen men aboard it is riding dangerously low in the water. The mutineers tossed in a few pounds of pork and a couple of containers of water, and not much more. Bligh and his men are facing almost certain death at sea.

For the next six weeks they survive fierce storms and attacks from hostile Pacific Islanders when they try to touch shore. But the most serious threat to their lives comes from starvation and thirst and it takes Bligh's disciplined rationing to make their meagre provisions last.

At one point, one man stands up in desperation and challenges Bligh, rejecting his authority. Bligh rises to his feet, places his hand on his cutlass, and faces the challenger down.

In six weeks, Bligh navigates the small craft over 5,800 kilometres, to the island of Timor. Not only does he deliver all but one of his men safely to this harbour, he continues to write his log and even to draw rough maps of the north coast of Australia.

We have skimmed over the past months, and now skip even more rapidly over the coming twelve years.

Here, briefly, is what happens:

In 1790, Bligh faces a court martial in England for 'losing' HMS *Bounty*. This naval court finds him not guilty of any wrongdoing.

In 1791, Bligh is promoted to the rank of captain and given command of HMS *Providence*. His immediate task is to transport breadfruit to the West Indies, and this time he accomplishes his mission.

In 1793, three of the *Bounty* mutineers are publicly hanged on board a ship on the Thames. Only a small number were ever captured because most left Tahiti and sailed on the *Bounty* to Pitcairn Island.

In 1801, Bligh is made a member of the Royal Society (that's a big deal!), for distinguished services to navigation and botany. Since his return, he has enjoyed a mixed reputation, with most people admiring him for his amazing seamanship but many steering clear of him since the execution of the mutineers.

In 1805, Bligh is appointed Governor of New South Wales.

In Sydney, the authority of the governor has been weakened and Bligh is determined to follow orders from London to re-establish it. The previous governor, Philip Gidley King, opened the doors of Government House to a stream of influential people who were pressing their claims for further privileges in the colony. In failing health, King found it increasingly hard to resist them.

Some of these influential people are military men, officers of the New South Wales Corps. Many have been using positions of authority to increase their own wealth, instead of attending to their duty of supporting the governor in maintaining law and order. In fact, many have been aggressively breaking the law by buying rum and other spirits cheaply and trading them at enormous profit. This trade is so rife that rum, and not the English pound, has become the main currency in the colony. The New South Wales military have well and truly earned their nickname, the Rum Corps.

But rum is only part of the story: the old British model of New South Wales as a government-run prison camp is cracking. An emerging class of enterprising businessmen see the colony as a land of endless opportunities to increase their wealth and influence. Governor Bligh has the task of restoring the old order and these entrepreneurs are his natural enemies. He attempts to rein in their profiteering and their land grabs.

Soon the new social and political elite of New South Wales mounts a campaign of opposition to the governor. The social media of the time – gossip, printed pamphlets and handbills – refer to him as 'Bounty Bligh' and ask whether there is a Christian in the colony who will stand up to this 'tyrant'.

Well, the Fletcher Christian of New South Wales turns out to be an ex-army officer called John Macarthur. Heavily involved in the illegal rum trade, Macarthur is a quarrelsome individual who has been at the centre of many conflicts in the colony – including a couple of deadly duels. He is consumed by private ambition and is as stubborn as Bligh himself.

COWPASTURES
government's PRIME cattle Run

Macarthur has a vision for a self-supporting colony based on a flourishing wool industry. He needs land on which to run his sheep, but Bligh does not share his vision and does not intend supporting him. Macarthur goes over his head, straight to London, and secures 2,000 hectares of land at a place known as Cowpastures. Bligh is furious because Cowpastures is the government's prime cattle run.

"2,000 hectares please"....

Macarthur and Bligh lock horns over a number of issues. When the governor orders the removal of private dwellings built on government land, Macarthur 'tweets' that Bligh is a threat to all private property in the colony. When a convict escapes aboard a ship sailing from Sydney, Macarthur refuses to pay a fine he is liable for as owner of that ship. Bligh has him arrested and jailed. Naked tyranny from Bounty Bligh!

GOVERNMENTLAND

This anti-Bligh campaign is working well in certain sections of the population, but the new governor is popular in other quarters, especially amongst those he assisted with flood relief in the Hawkesbury region. Macarthur is such a skilful operator, however, that he manages to convince the commander of the New South Wales Corps, Major George Johnston, that there is widespread unrest in the colony. They are on the brink of a major, bloody revolution! They must rid themselves of this tyrant before it is too late!

And that brings us back to Government House on 26 January 1808, where Bligh is being marched downstairs, a prisoner of Major Johnston's men. The story quickly spreads that Bligh had to be hauled out from his hiding place under a bed, proof that the tyrant is really a coward! Not long afterwards a painting appears showing this version of the event and it soon becomes part of the anti-Bligh propaganda. This picture is regarded as the first-ever political cartoon produced in Australia.

Whether Bligh is hiding because he is afraid or is simply avoiding capture until he can escape to the Hawkesbury, the important thing to remember is that this is a huge – and unique – moment in Australian history. We are talking about an armed rebellion in which the military, urged on by men with certain political and business interests, overthrow a government headed by the king's appointed representative. This mutinous event has become known as the Rum Rebellion but, as we have seen, it was about much more than rum.

What happened to the major players in this drama? By 1810 Major Johnston, John Macarthur and William Bligh are in London. Johnston is court-martialled for his part in the rebellion, found guilty, dismissed from the army, then, much to Bligh's disgust, allowed to return to his property in New South Wales. Macarthur escapes trial altogether. He eventually returns home to continue his prominent involvement in the wool industry and politics. William Bligh, this man who once longed to be captain, is promoted to rear admiral, a rank he holds until his death from cancer in 1817.

So, what are we to make of William Bligh, the man at the centre of two famous mutinies? We are not going to fall for the myth of Bligh, the brutish bully of the *Bounty*, for we know – as Macarthur well knew – that simple slogans and labels are meant to stop us thinking any further about things.

There is no doubt that Bligh left himself open to criticism for he did not fit the traditional image of an officer and a gentleman: he had a fierce temper and a savage tongue. Maybe he did not understand that ranting, raving and swearing lessened, rather than increased, his authority. But what he lacked in gentlemanly reserve he made up for with an energetic enthusiasm to obey and enforce orders and a conscientious concern for the welfare of those under his command.

'traitors'
Rebels'
you have just
walked over my husband's grave.
now you come to murder my father!
Kill me if you will but spare my father!

We might conclude that Bligh simply sailed into challenges that were far too complex for a man of his background and training. For what was he to do when he and his crew found themselves 'marooned' for five months on a tropical island? What naval regulations existed to deal with the sunny seductions of such a paradise?

When Bligh arrived in New South Wales he found a society already shrugging off Old World views of colonial life; in this New World his tough, uncompromising insistence on obedience was too simplistic. He needed a more flexible approach to governing and a more forward-looking understanding of what was happening around him.

A more flexible and forward-looking approach to governing arrived in New South Wales in 1809 with William Bligh's successor, Lachlan Macquarie.

But that's another story…

W. BLIGH
one who has integrity
unimpeached, a mind
capable of providing resources
without leaning on
others.
firm in discipline
civil independent
and not subject to
whim or whine when
severity of
discipline is wanted
to meet
emergencies

Loyalist No 1.

Read the other books in the series.

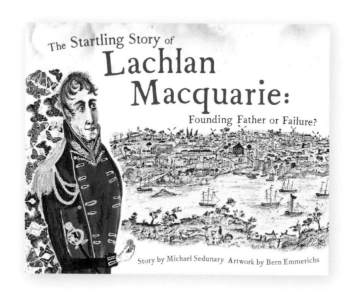

The Startling Story of
Lachlan Macquarie:
Founding Father or Failure?

Story by Michael Sedunary Artwork by Bern Emmerichs

The Unlikely Story of
Bennelong and Phillip
by Michael Sedunary   Artwork by Bern Emmerichs

What's your story?
by Rose Giannone   Artwork by Bern Emmerichs

BERBAY
PUBLISHING

www.berbaybooks.com